Changing Your (Virtue Reality)

Discovering And Displaying The Virtuous Woman In You

Written by – Minister Sandra Patrick
Book 1 Authentication

Contents

Forward

It is not a common occurrence to know a person like Sandra Patrick a true minister of the Kingdom of God! She is a true promoter of the kingdom of Heaven principles and this book is on the cutting edge of that way of thinking and living. It is not only the words that are in this book but the real-life application that is promoted. Sandra Patrick first book of this series leave you wanting to hear more for this amazing woman of God! Let this virtual Reality be yours through her writing. The true clear leading of the Holy Spirit of God is seen in the wisdom of this book she authored. Following the words of King Lemuel Mother as he describes her portrayal of the virtuous woman in the book of proverbs. I believe that you will be enriched as you read and commit to these words in this book Virtuality (Virtue Reality)!

Kevin N. Steward – An Apostle of Jesus Christ

Pastor of Living Bread Church International World-Wide Ministries

Author of the Book "Getting Understanding Volume 1: Women in Ministry – Empowering Today's Women"

and many other books.

Acknowledgements

Writing has been for me, a dream come true. Since I was a child, I've always been fascinated with writing. Little did I know that I would be writing for the Kingdom of God. It is still difficult for me to contain my excitement about writing. God knew all along what He had placed in me and trusted me to bring it to pass. I thank God and give Him glory, honor, and praise for giving me the persistence and courage to put pen to paper.

What would life be without the support of family and friends? First and foremost, I'd like to acknowledge my wonderful husband, Derek, who has been extremely patient and kind to me during the beginning stages of this project. His support was steady throughout the seemingly never-ending hours that were necessary for me to devote to studying, reading, and writing to complete this, the first of many to come. Thank you! To all the children God entrusted me with, born of us or given to us for a season, thank you for remaining fixed on the sidelines, cheering me on with your input and your loving kindness. To all my family, especially my brother Kevin whose technical assistance made this process understandable, and to my sisters, those in my class, my family, lifelong friendship and the Butterfly Ladies thank you for being a fortress around me. To my mom, the smartest person I know, thank you for never placing limits on my dreams. Last, but certainly not least, to my mother-in-law, thank you for laboring with me to fully understand God's generosity. All of you have been stellar examples of what God love is, and I appreciate the jewels that you are in my life. Thank you, all, for your love and encouragement.

Introduction

"This above all: to thine own self be true," William Shakespeare

There was a time in my life and on my journey that for approximately a year or more, I referred to God as, Jehovah Roi, which means, The God who sees Me. This title, Jehovah Roi, is more commonly attributed to Hagar's reference in the story of Hagar and Ishmael during her and her son's desert experience. It was during this time in my life that I, like Hagar, had been cast out and left without resources. I can remember that during that season, I had committed my heart, mind, and soul to whatever I did, good or bad, and I continued to lift my eyes to heaven and say, Father, you see me. This was a time when I freely submitted my life to God and patiently waited on Him to give me instructions. This is a pretty way of saying that I was stuck, stubborn, broken, literally with a broken foot and was out of fellowship with the church. Most desert experiences aren't very pretty. When God did speak, He gave me these words, ***"I have been at work in you to will and to do, according to my good pleasure."*** This experience was necessary to receive God's assurance. Therefore, what started out with me feeling that I was an outcast and a misfit, God introduced me to the understanding that I was peculiar, uniquely designed and accomplished in His sight.

For the purposes of this book the word Virtuality and Virtue Reality are defined as, the essence of the new creation in Christ Jesus who you have become. Also, it encompasses the fact that there is an unseen change in you that may lack acknowledgment in the world, church, your family, workplace or even within your own mind, emotions, and actions. It refers to the foreordained, prophetic, and present evidence of God's interaction, direction, and purpose for your life. It also aligns with scripture and in this case specifically Provers 31:10-31.

These books are written so that each of the 20 Characteristics are thoroughly discussed in each chapter with each of the 5-books covering the characteristics pertaining to that manifestation of God's movement in your life. For example, the first book is Authentication and covers the first 2 characteristics pertaining to her personally defined traits.

This book is also intended to become your journal in which you, the reader, can chronicle your journey with God though this process. Prayerfully, the book will become your working document for identifying your inner abilities that reflect the woman who the Bible describes as the one woman that is more excellent than them all. Please note that the importance of knowing how much God has invested in you, this is importance because of the demand that is presently coming on the Body of Christ to present our bodies as living sacrifices. The demand from God upon our lives is to display the evidence of His kingship in the earth. Much like the early church, which endured persecution because of their faith, we must be willing to openly declare our faith in this world's spiritual, financial, social, mental, and physical climate. Eventually, we will see the following statement ringing true: *"...The kingdoms of this world have become the kingdoms of our Lord and of His Christ...,*[1]*"*

It is my hope that as you read these words, they will assist you in your daily walk with God and I am praying that this kingdom message is clear, and that it brings validation and vindication to those who have not seen their reflection through the redemptive mirror of God's holy presence. It is the first step in unlocking the mystery that is the virtuous woman in you and changing your Virtuality that is your personal acknowledgement of the reality of your hard-won virtuous qualities. Through this book, God is going to show you how he has been creating an epic story with your name on it. I have interpreted it into a workable text, even though each characteristic is lengthy, it is important to focus on the essence of each of them. Prayerfully this will help us hear God's voice. I believe that this is the way that God sees his virtuous daughters.

Also take the time to journal. There is no time limit, and there is no right or wrong answer. It is meant to be a journey that you take with the Father, Son and Holy Spirit so you can discuss your authenticity. It is also meant to document all of the abilities you have gained through all life experiences good and bad, happy, and sad, easy, and difficult. Life has given you confidence and bears witness to your active faith in the past, present, and future. Recording these events will bring glory to the praise of God's grace and document the evidence of His Love at work in you. So, take your time, be introspective and create a written manifesto of God's ability to work in you. Now Read Proverb 31: 10-31 in any version of your choice.

---

[1] Revelations 11:15

Journal Page - Activity: Write down your thought and comments from Reading Proverb 31:10-31.

_____

_____

_____

_____

_____

_____

_____

_____

_____

_____

_____

_____

_____

_____

_____

_____

_____

_____

_____

_____

_____

_____

_____

_____

Part 1 Owning it.

Characteristic I – Handcrafted by the Master Potter

> *Every block of stone has a statue inside it, and it is the task of the sculptor to discover it. Michelangelo*

"She is intelligent, capable, virtuous, spiritually discerning, able to choose the good portion, resourceful and industrious. Her presence is uniquely desirable, and her worth is not measured by the current market rate of precious stones, for she has proven to be much more valuable. "

Life is a continual onslaught of stuff. In my experiences, and perhaps those who read my books, know that there will always be challenges in life. If you are raising children, working inside or outside of the home, helping your elderly parents, or dealing with a new or growing business, you've got stuff happening every day. During these times, we need God to intervene on our behalf. Our fervent plea in these situations may sound like, Lord, how will you get the glory out of this?

We don't always see God's point of view during the lessons of life. In the movie *The Karate Kid*, I'm referring to the 1984 version with Ralph Macchio, the story line revolves around a kid, who was drilled into executing a repetitive motion. It is not until later in the movie that the drill becomes an ingrained habit which proves to be invaluable to his defense. Just like the kid in the movie, we tend to remain stagnant in our challenges. We are constantly pleading to the Lord, why am I still in this same place, same job, same church, same unproductive relationship, or same home? Our behavior mimics the kid in that, even though we look to the master to teach us what we need, we still question the technique God uses to teach us.

In Proverbs 31:10-31, we see a description and model of the virtuous woman. As I examined myself, I have always felt like those virtues are well beyond my reach, or it would be impossible for me to be so skilled. This high degree of virtue reminds me of the actress Barbara Billingsley, who played June Cleaver in the1950's sitcom, *Leave It to Beaver*. She and her husband portrayed the archetypal suburban parents of two sons. June was always clad in a pearl necklace, and in the early afternoon, she was seen vacuuming her home. Her life was characterized as the consummate wife and tidy mother.

There was absolutely no depiction of her having to deal with real life issues such as baby poop, unruly children, nor did she ever enter into a room where an aged parent required tending. It was fiction at its finest. However, the Proverbs 31 woman is not fiction. The following represents a breakdown of the scripture so that we can see just how much we have in common with this valuable woman. She is an authentic vessel having been molded in the furnace of life by the hands of the Master potter. She is the physical representation of his desire, an instrument fit for the Maker and designed to accomplish the task he has assigned her to.

Changing Your Virtuality (Virtue Reality)

As you identify the unique ways that God has given you skills and insight, you will understand the correct definition of authentic. Like Websters Dictionary definition you will discover You are the real deal. Webster state that authentic means "Real, Actual Not false or imitation", "true to one's own personality, spirit or character," also "worthy of acceptance or belief as conforming to or based on fact". May I add that no devil or enemy of God; no prison, real or imagined; no sickness or disability can prevent God from using you in the authentic life you have been prepared for. As we begin to dissect the points of characteristic one (1), make sure you do the journal assignment afterwards, as it is an important part of the journey towards the recognition of your authentication.

Changing Your Virtuality (Virtue Reality)

She is Intelligent

"A mind is a terrible thing to waste." -- Arthur Fletcher

Let's define intelligence. Intelligence is a general mental ability due to the integrative and adaptive functions of the brain that permit complex, un-stereotyped, purposive responses to novel or changing situations, involving discrimination, generalization, learning, concept formation, inference, mental manipulation of memories, images, words and abstract symbols, education of relations and correlates, reasoning, and problem solving.[2] Wow. That's a mouth full!

Here is an everyday example. My mother, one of the smartest people I know, loves to do crossword puzzles. She also watches shows like *Jeopardy* and *Wheel of Fortune*. These are gameshows that test one's intelligence. In all the years I have observed her, she casually answers the difficult questions. With that being said, I've never heard her say, Gee, I must be intelligent. Yet, she demonstrates a profound competency that certainly surpasses my brain waves. My mother solves complex problems after dinner for fun. With all this intellectual prowess, my mother does not possess an advanced degree. She was able to use her intelligence to raise five (5) children, several nieces, nephews, and other relatives, even though she was a single parent. Surely, God gifted her with a kind of intelligence that was full of compassion.

---

[2] McGraw Science and Technology dictionary, (2005)

Changing Your Virtuality (Virtue Reality)

During the course of your life, you may find yourself saying, I don't have a high school diploma, or you may say, I have 3 degrees, and I'm still unemployed. It is safe to conclude that your problem may not be a lack of education. Yet, you may find that every time you say something, people look at you as though you're speaking another language. Or when you finish a day of chasing and tending to your children, your house still looks like you didn't do one thing. In all that stuff, God is giving you experiences that will eventually become a fluid motion that will defeat the enemy. At this point, you might be saying, Yeah, but you just don't know how bad it is for me. To that notion, I say, Ha! Here's why.

In a particularly difficult period of my life, I brought a house for $1 from the city of Detroit, Michigan. Now, one may say that was good. However, here's some inside information that would make one rethink that it was a good thing. The contractor I hired to rehab the one-dollar house, took one look at it, then looked at me and asked, who is going to live here? To make matters worse, the house was located in a colorful and interesting or seedy and dilapidated part of town. The house had been abandoned for years and was part of one of Detroit's programs to revitalize the city as well as to increase homeownership. Even with that objective the program's process made you jump through so many hoops and deal with all kinds of red tape it almost made you want to give up. However, all the things that I learned about real estate, local government, city ordinances, program compliance and the loan process proved to be priceless in my life. We would eventually sell real estate, run a youth program in the City with City funding and accomplish our dream of helping youth to change their outlook. As I said, I obtained all of this information during a very difficult and stressful time in my life, having to care for my children, while staying with my mom, marriage in shambles, and dealing with an extreme amount of weight gain - God still used me and those experiences still helps me to this very day.

During that season in my life there was this 3–4-year separation from my husband. Prayer was the only way I was able to release all of the anguish, trouble, fear, hurt, confusion, and desperation in my life. After moving in our new home, with my four small children I started and successfully operated my own daycare. To add to the divinely organized chaos in my life, as if I needed more, I also operated a small tax practice – all this while looking for a church home. My children would hear me, in the basement at 3:00 a.m., crying out to the Lord. In that solitude, I learned how to spend time with the Lord and how to depend on Him. Most importantly I learned how to be broken in spirit.[3] The basement floor became my thrashing floor – a place where the Lord dealt with the hard and unyielding part of my life and my heart. He addressed the deep injuries I had sustained and help me surrender them bit by bit. It wasn't fun or easy. But in those days, I learned that I am a true believer, a worshiper, and a daughter of God. Just keeping my wits about myself

---

[3] Psalms 51:17

was a gift from heaven above. Negotiating life under distress takes intelligence.

Changing Your Virtuality (Virtue Reality)

(Journal Page) – Activity – Write down your own definition of Intelligence. Then name five intelligent things about you. Think on it.

_____

_____

_____

_____

_____

_____

_____

_____

_____

_____

_____

_____

_____

_____

_____

_____

_____

_____

_____

_____

_____

She is Capable

"Necessity is the mother of invention." – Plato

Being capable means that you can do something, and you have the ability to perform a task or do many various things well. In order to be capable, you don't have to have a license or even a particular make up; it's what the Lord gave you.

I once saw a YouTube video about a lady who made quilts. At first, I thought, here's one of those people who wants to show off their handcraft skills. So, I watched it and began to see that this lady was an entrepreneur who had just learned to sew. She used to be a radio personality and had now become a stay-at-home quilter.

What could make her change professions so drastically? Eventually, it was revealed that she was blind. Incredible, right? But how does a blind woman sew? Understandably, it would be logical if she had just given up. Why didn't she just give up and become limited to a certain lifestyle that would complement her disability? Instead, her answer was a definite no to bow down to her new limitation. This very capable woman stated that she asked God what to do, and He told her that she should use her hands, and then He showed her how she should use her hands.

Soon after that revelation, she met a lady who asked her if she could quilt. Her response was no. The lady then asked, "Would you like to learn?" She replied, "Yes." I don't know if the teacher realized that her new pupil was blind, but it seemed obvious to me that there would be some challenges. However, this was the beginning of a new journey for a faithful woman of God. This one-time celebrity radio personality, who had experienced great success in one arena, became a wonderful businesswoman in a totally different arena, as a quilter, and now she is a witness and a true testament as to how God can give you abundance [4] no matter what obstacles you face.

One problem with our lifestyles and daily activities is that we are often cast into situations that have nothing to do with our God-given talents. Can you imagine a factory worker whose real talent is to be an artist? Or can you imagine a person who lost their way, to drugs and a depraved life, who should have been a schoolteacher? Identifying your natural skills will give you a glimpse of the possibilities that lie in your future. I love the movie *Family Man* with Nicholas Cage. In this story, an egocentric, unscrupulous, narcissistic, go-getter must live life as a husband, father and tire salesman. The beauty of the story is that he eventually realizes what is truly important in life. Love and fidelity, friendship and loyalty and parenthood, can give you what life in the fast lane could never give you. I believe that as we continue to journey through the characteristics of the virtuous woman, God will give you insights into the possibilities that are right there inside of you.

---

[4] John 10:10

Changing Your Virtuality (Virtue Reality)

(Journal Page) – Activity- Name several things that you love to do. Please do not limit this to employment. Be sure to include things like shopping, making sandcastles, coloring or anything that gives you joy. Then identify one way in which you could make money doing this thing for a living. Don't worry if it hasn't been done before. Be innovative, and whatever it is, DO NOT consider it stupid.

_____

_____

_____

_____

_____

_____

_____

_____

_____

_____

_____

_____

_____

_____

_____

_____

_____

_____

_____

She is Virtuous

"Let us always meet each other with a smile, for a smile
is the beginning of love." – Mother Teresa

Let's put this out there. The virtuous woman is not necessarily a virgin or was a virgin at the time she got married. I remember always thinking of Mother Theresa a nun who vows lifelong celibacy as a commitment to God as the consummate example of a virtuous woman. After my sojourn in life, coming back to the Lord with children and no husband, I resigned myself to thinking that's something I would never be able to accomplish. I felt like I had blown that a long time ago. But I understood that being virtuous, which means discerning, or having high standards, is a different matter. Frankly, the point is not to take away your past. Your past is where you met God and came to know a type of desperation and need for the born-again life. It allowed you to open your heart to the Holy Spirit for healing and correction so that those experiences prepared you to meet your future.

Some of you reading this book may have said to yourselves, I have a million-dollar taste and a ten-dollar wallet. The truth is you have million-dollar wishes and ten-dollar faith. Everything you have experienced is needed to grow your faith from an immature whining child to a mature child of the Living God. Then as a mature child with faith you can speak to mountains and cause them to throw themselves into the sea![5] Confusion or and immaturity starts in-part because we let others minimize some or all of the skills and ability that God has given us – the ones He has revealed bit by bit during seasons of difficulties and trials. We also look to other for our self-worth especially if our past is filled with mistakes, errors, and sin. The enemy will continue to use our doubt and others cruel words to keep us in the dark place of anguish, stress, and pain. It's very difficult to grow if you can't feel the Son's light.

For example, as a young woman, after the purchase, rehab and sell of my $1 house, I lived near an exclusive part of town that had very high-end stores. I would say to my friends, let's go to the stores over in the Park, but they would say that they were too expensive! Well, I ventured there with my girls.

I loved the way the store sounded, all quiet and ethereal. They had the smell of a lightly floral fragrance and looked like the Taj Mahal. I would browse the shop as if I had the right to be there, just as anyone else did. It was this experience that taught me about buying in the off season. The same quality-made clothes were priced lower so I could afford them. This provided me with the ability to dress my family well. Some women's experiences have included the discovery of resale shops. These and similar experiences opened new avenues that satisfied the need for clothing, yet at the same time provided the opportunity to dress like a queen. Others have learned to sew, barter, and go to garage sales or use

---

[5] Mark 11:23

other avenues to get things done and meet their needs. These are the individuals who possess a drive in them that causes them to see and choose the good portion of things available no matter where those items may be. She can see pass the price tags, piles of clothes, mountains of discarded items to get to the best items available and needed for her household. I have to share with you the story of the long green comfortable couch.

During the time my family and I lived in our one-dollar house we were in need of many things. One of them was furniture. I didn't really pray for a long green comfortable couch, but God knew what we needed. As I was driving home one morning after dropping my son Eric off at school, I saw a couch sitting on the side of the road. By the way I have found many good items on the side of the road, left just for me. Anyway, this couch was a massive 8 feet long or at least it seemed that way. I pulled over to examine this jewel sitting there for the taking. I walked around it, no holes, no tears, not even any worn spots. I'll take it I thought. Oh, there's one problem. No one to help me lift it or tie it to the roof of my car. What to do I thought? Then, I just spoke to the angel that is always with me. I said, you get one side and I'll get this side. So, me and the angel, that I did not see, but he was there, for he helped me lift the couch, put it on top of the car without any thing to secure it, and I drove it the 10 or so blocks home. When we got to our house the same guardian angel helped me lift the couch off the car and sit it in the backyard where I could put it until my husband came home. Well, the rest of this story is history, but you could not imagine how my husband looked at me when I told him that the angel and I brought this home on the car with nothing holding it down. The thing that got me was I could not move the couch one we got it home. The angel task was done I suppose. So, my husband and my sons moved the long couch into the house with many grunts and groans and astonishment that I was even able to move such a beast. By the way that couch was our family furniture until we moved three years later. I had chosen a good piece of furniture in spite of where I gathered it from.

In the Christian community, we often quote the scripture say, ***"God will give you the desire of your heart,"***[6] but in contrast to that saying, we hold on to things that we do not love, want, or need. We cling to the familiar, while we keep our hands figuratively behind our backs. I am asking each person to lift your hands to God and ask Him to fill them with purpose and ability. Implore God to line up your actions (dollars) with your faith (taste). Ask Him to clarify your talents and to work on your mind, thoughts, and emotions, so you can be who He made you to be and accomplish what he sent you to do.

---

[6] Psalm 37:4

Changing Your Virtuality (Virtue Reality)

Journal Page – Activity – Name five women you believe to be virtuous. Write their names down. Then, if possible, call them and ask how they maintained their standards in life.

_____

_____

_____

_____

_____

_____

_____

_____

_____

_____

_____

_____

_____

_____

She is Resourceful

"Only I can change my life. No one can do it for me." –
Carrol Burnet

I love this one. This is one of the first attributes that the Lord taught me. I was in high school, and I had a co-op teacher that gave us an exercise one day in class. We had to quickly tell her a number of things. Well, me being me, I immediately started by flipping through the book we were reading, to locate some of the answers. At that point, she stopped the class and diverted the class's attention in my direction. She said, Look at Sandra, She is resourceful. From that moment on, those words have always resounded so firmly in my heart, life, and soul.

I have been able to use this talent to produce a living even without money. Have you ever met a person who you knew was unemployed, not doing any illegal or immoral things, but always had plenty? I think of a particular friend in this case. She lived at levels that I could only dream of. But everyplace she lived, the house was well kept with flowers or a garden, and there was always a lot of activity.

I remember when unemployment was at an all-time high back in the 1980's and many families had to turn to government assistance. Well, it was not the neediest or the smartest people that got through that system. It was the ones who were resourceful. One must be savvy in order to navigate through a system that was designed to degrade and deny benefits more times than not. There was a certain way in which people needed to be resourceful in order to get the goods.

Changing Your Virtuality (Virtue Reality)

Before moving on, I want you to understand that the benevolent acts of our government are to provide for the general welfare of its citizens through government assistance. Like God's Kingdom every citizen has the benefit of being under the care of the King. This grace is a constitutional component in our society, and I believe that the majority of people use it to smooth out rough seasons in their lives. I said that to say, it is unfortunate however, that some of the resourceful people, those who have mastered the complicated labyrinth of paperwork it takes to receive assistance, continue to repeatedly go back to the system once they have learned how to milk the proverbial cow. They fail or refuse to see it as a temporary solution. As a result, they have been economically and psychologically stuck for years.

One of the most important lessons, I'd hope for you to glean from this section, is that you can't have anything more than milk in life if you settle for milk[7]. For example, using government assistance, the individuals who are talented enough to be resourceful become limited because they settle for a temporary comfort zone or condition. If only they could realize that this talent could give them access to a land flowing with milk and honey.[8] Let me share with you a story about one of my girlfriends. I have known this person since I was 20 yrs. old. Over the years we've discussed many things about our lives, challenges, families, dreams, and spiritual conditions. As time passed my friend

---

[7] Hebrews 5:13
[8] Exodus 3:8

found herself at a crossroads in her career. She could either continue to work at a clerical level or pursue her degree and aim for higher responsibility in a different field. So, she made the decision to go back to college to pursue her bachelor's degree. She encountered some negativity because of her age but also, she had feelings of being overwhelmed with new technology and the pace at which they expected you to finish each class. She questioned herself about the benefits of a degree, the financial responsibility, and most of all the uncertainty of breaking into a new field and getting a good job. Long story short, she got the degree, with a little hand holding, and later the job. God knew all the time that the talent was in her and that her resourcefulness to get assistance and overcome barriers would cause her to succeed. She decided to leave her comfort zone to receive the rewards that come with letting go of the old and embracing the new. She gladly let go of the watered down, constraining, and cumbersome milk that she initially drank and receive the milk and honey of land of overcomers.

Changing Your Virtuality (Virtue Reality)

Journal page - Activity – List three things you would wish for if you were stranded on a desert island. As you consider those things, describe how those things would make a difference in your life.

_____

_____

_____

_____

_____

_____

_____

_____

_____

_____

_____

_____

_____

_____

_____

_____

She is Industrious

"Where you go, I will go, and where you stay, I will stay." (Ruth 1:16, NIV)

Does the word industrious make you think of Janitor in the Drum, an old industrial-strength cleaner that destroyed all the dirt in its way? Well, in a sense, this characteristic strongly implies that an individual possesses the ability, above and beyond the norm, to break through barriers that would otherwise stop or discourage them.

Have you ever read the book *The Little Red Hen*? As a child, this was one of my favorite books. The hen found the seed. That would be you, the person reading this. She asked those around her for help. Did she get any? No, she did not. The dog and cat gave all kinds of excuses because they couldn't help with the planting and the tending and the milling and the baking. But as soon as the bread was done, who was at the table waiting for their portion? Should the little red hen have forgiven everyone for their laziness and just given away her bread? Here's a biblical analogy. Consider the five wise virgins in the book of Matthew chapter 25 verse 7-9. Did they give their oil away? No. Would you?

One reason why some people don't have as much as they should have, is because they lean on their own understanding. In other words, they only trust what is in their own realm of reference and experience. This can result in their denial to accept new information. Why? Because it supersedes the familiar, which creates discomfort. These are the individuals who constantly give their talents and treasures away to people who don't deserve it. Now, I'm not saying that your children or your dependents must work for everything they get, but some things should only be gained through the work of that individual. You might think that is a hard position to take but it's a real one.

Answer these questions, should I get part of your paycheck? or should I wait on your doorstep for you to come from the grocery store so I can fill my cabinets? Would you put up with me expecting to benefit from your labor without being a part of the work? Please do not misunderstand me. We are not talking about merely giving to a causes that we believe in. We all give in many ways for many reasons. We give to less fortunate people, families, friends, parents, and humanitarian causes. What I am speaking about is the talent that yields an abundance of fruit.

Child of God, you are a captain of industry in some form or fashion. It doesn't matter if it's at the local school, church, volunteer position, in the board room, or on the factory floor. Have you found the place where your hands can produce fruit? Not an apple unless you are an Orchardist. But fruit, in the sense of items produced by your own ingenuity, abilities and energy. Now let me pose this question: Is the ground that you're tilling the ground you should be tilling? Has God shown you that you should be working on something else or someplace else?

Let's take this thought further. Ask yourself this question: Why am I producing a lot, but still unable to make my ends meet? As I'm writing this, I'm thinking of the person who is saying to themselves, I don't have anything, or I'm depressed or I'm sick and tired of being sick and tired.

Let me stop you right there, because you are at the right place, you are not alone. Those who will be honest can admit being where you are right now. It is almost a prerequisite to learn how to submit to God. We must get to this point in life or in our journey with God to be desperate enough to give up our ways, ideas, and reasoning. Why? Because we finally and sincerely will look to God, realizing that our own abilities, schemes, and intellect are no longer working or even sufficient to address our issues. The good news is that God has always had a way of escape[9] for us and He lifts us up to a higher level of life when we turn to Him[10].

Let's look at Naomi in the book of Ruth. Naomi was the mother of two sons, and she had a good husband. Ruth was her daughter-in-law. In her culture, her status almost guaranteed that she would be secure for life. She and her family relocated to another town. She was able to see her sons get married. It appeared that, Naomi was living the life. Then tragedy struck. Naomi's husband died, and thereafter, both of her sons died. Almost in an instance, both of her daughters-in-law became widows. Seeing no value in them remaining with her after the death of

---

[9] 1Corthians 10:13
[10] John 10:10

her sons, Naomi told her daughters-in-law to return to their pre-marital homes. Naomi seemingly lost everything and eventually returned to her hometown with nothing, yet she was unable to shake the accompanying presence of her daughter-in-law, Ruth. She is Naomi's constant reminder of her loss.

Now a grieving Naomi, changes her name to Mara, which means bitter[11]. Can you imagine being so sad that you don't want anyone to call you by the name you had when things were good? Grieving so much that it hurts to think about lost loved ones? I don't know about you, but I felt sorry for Naomi. Thank God for Ruth, as she was the person who remained by Naomi's side. Ruth was industrious and obedient to her mother-in-law. She worked to provide for them, and she obeyed her mother-in-law[12].

In the end, because of Ruth's obedience in using her industrious gift, she became the great-great grandmother of David, a direct descendant in the genealogical lineage of our Lord and savior Jesus Christ. If life has been devastating for you, then ask God to identify your industrious qualities or send you an industrious person. Like the blind quilter ask God to give you a different type of sight and new abilities. If life has been good and you still don't have enough, ask God if you should be more like the little red hen or the five virgins. If you have

---

[11] Ruth 1:19-21
[12] Ruth 3:5

everything you need but your soul is not satisfied ask God for forgiveness and then listen for his instructions.

Changing Your Virtuality (Virtue Reality)

Journal Page – Activity – Draw an organization chart that identifies all the responsibilities you have to perform (ministry, business and personal) to get thing done in a timely manner. Then pray and ask God to show you how to become industrious so you can accomplish your goals. Don't forget to ask for help and support in arears where you feel overwhelmed.

She is Uniquely Desirable

"I'm not offended by the dumb blond jokes because I know I'm not dumb and I also know I'm not blond." – Dolly Parton

Have you ever been around a person who everybody seems to love? It's as though that person possesses this indescribable ability to draw in a crowd. This individual is able to make everyone in the crowd feel special. Many people expressed that Princess Diana had this kind of presence, which probably earned her the title of "People's Princess.[13]" Most of us may not consider ourselves as beautiful, rich, or charismatic as Princess Di, but there are people you do know who have that same ability. What is most important about being desired is to find the place where your talent naturally flows.

For example, not too long ago, we had a penny war at work. This war was a fund-raising effort where the employees got into teams and each team had to fill a water cooler bottle full of pennies. That was the easy part. They then had to put silver coins in their opponent's bottles because silver reduced the penny count in the end. Team leaders emerged who did not normally function in that capacity at work. If you can imagine some of the people, one in particular influenced, led, and encouraged her team to raise money by sneaking silver into the other teams' bottle. We were all amazed at the transformation of this

---

[13]https://www.cnn.com/2020/08/31/world/princess-diana-death-the-windsors-series/index.html

individual, as she was truly gifted to team lead. It was clear that she was in her element. In that arena, her presence and skills were needed, and everyone appreciated seeing her natural gifts flourish.

On the opposite end of this spectrum are those who the devil oppresses such that they will never know their true self.

The classic fairy tale of Cinderella shows how a person can see the truth about you, do everything in their ability to oppress you and prevent you from knowing how unique a person that you are. It was only when the princess was allowed to be her best self that she accepted her own value. After that, she automatically garnered the attention of everyone around her, including the most important person in the room, the prince.

You may scoff at this example and say, "Well, honey, I'm not living in a fairy tale. This is real life, and it is tough." My response to that is, what or who is keeping you from knowing how unique you are? In the fairy tell it was the evil stepmother or some might even say it was the blinded father who let the evil person in. Even though God is not a fairy God Father he is a caring and loving parent. The scripture said he spared not his only son so we might have everlasting life[14]. Remember God is the God of the living[15] and he give good gifts to those who believe[16]. Ask him to give you favor with man and God[17] so your own

---

[14] John 3:16
[15] Matthew 22:32-34

uniqueness can reflect his glory and illuminate any room or place you enter.

---

[16] Matthew 7:11
[17] Proverbs 3:4

Changing Your Virtuality (Virtue Reality)

Journal Page - Activity – Write a short paragraph about a time when you were overwhelmed by someone else's presence. Then write another paragraph depicting a time when people were overwhelmed by your presence. If you can't think of a time, write a fairy tale about yourself.

Changing Your Virtuality (Virtue Reality)

She has Unmeasured Worth

"In the flush of Love's light, we dare be brave and suddenly we see that love cost all we are and will ever be. Yet it is only love which set us free." – Maya Angelou

How do you measure the value of a human life? Well, for years you have heard people say, especially about women, that she's not worth a thing. They may be referring to the way a person cooks, works, invests money, or takes care of a household. Somewhere along the line, we became comfortable assessing the value of a person based on their behavior and our attitude. People are not perfect, but most do the best they can, to live a life that shows a triumphant sprit and an excellent attitude towards it.

How can you compare Harriett Tubman and the work she did during the Civil War to the value of currency? Many people don't know that not only was Mrs. Tubman the person who led many slaves to freedom, but that she also taught them to lead. She also was an intelligence gatherer for the General in the Northern (Union) army. Mrs. Tubman was as an unassuming person while infiltrating the enemy territory. How do you place a value on her courage, tenacity, concern, foresight, dedication, and selflessness? Without Mrs. Tubman, many who desired freedom would have gotten lost or have been captured in their pursuits. The irony of the situation is that many people thought of her as a slave, traitor, upstart, and many more unseemly words. We may salute her in history as a heroine, but in her time, she was hunted and had a bounty on her head. What diamonds, sapphires or gems can you compared to her? She was neither statuesque nor a great beauty, but she had the love of many. She lived a life that proved her worth. How do we compare to such a great woman?

If we live life to the best of our ability, whether that is full of mistakes or success, if we learn the lessons that cause us to improve with time then, and only then, will we see that God has been with us all along. The scriptures below provide us with step-by-step instructions on how to improve our attitude and outlook, it states,

> *"For this very reason, make every effort to add to your faith goodness; and to goodness, knowledge; and to knowledge, self-control; and to self-control, perseverance; and to perseverance, godliness; and to godliness, mutual affection; and to mutual affection, love. For if you possess these qualities in increasing measure, they will keep you from being ineffective and unproductive in your knowledge of our Lord Jesus Christ." (2 Peter 1:5-8 NIV)*

These steps will move you forward in changing and mastering your Virtue Reality (Virtuality).

Changing Your Virtuality (Virtue Reality)

Journal Page – Activity – Write a biography for yourself that shows your progress through the years of your family and significant relationship. Be sure to include good, bad, hard, and easy things.

_____

_____

_____

_____

_____

_____

_____

_____

_____

_____

_____

_____

_____

_____

_____

_____

_____

_____

_____

_____

_____

_____

Part 2 – Finding Hidden Treasure

Characteristic 2 – The Master has Left His Mark

"Every great dream begins with a dreamer. Always remember, you have within you the strength, the patience, and the passion to reach for the stars to change the world." –
Araminta Ross Green, known as Harriet Tubman

"Her relationship with her husband if she has one or God if she is single has been developed so that he totally trusts her decision to bring honor to him and your household. His confidence in her has been solidified through her ability to love, guide, and support his decisions in many endeavors. She helps him to choose honest and excellent ways and to avoid mistakes. Her ability to love, comfort and encourage him is done with all her strength, and he is envied by many for they see that she is very good to him."

Part of the mystery of the Proverbs 31 woman is that she is pictured as the best wife ever. The whole of the proverb is about how to find this woman, so she can be a wife. However, it does not give insight into her other status, meaning what she must have been before becoming a wife. She was a single woman at one time and a daughter, a student, a caregiver, and many other things. Surely, these are the arenas where God trained her how to be this excellent woman. So please don't say to yourself, *"I don't have a husband or the one I had is gone,"* but rather let's look at the characteristics of this woman and see how she is essentially an authentic daughter of the King.

She Brings Honor to her Household

"Carry out random acts of kindness with no expectation
of reward, safe in the knowledge that someday someone might
do the same for you." – Princess Diana

Relationships are just that – they are the way you relate to your kinfolk, co-workers, neighbors, church or religious congregants and other personal connections you have ties to. This woman has many people who she interacts with, but it is her kinfolk who are first blessed because of her presence. She has been through many ordeals, and despite her challenges, she has become more than a brilliant jewel.

It's funny how people may not know you, but they judge you by your spouse's or relatives' behavior. Haven't you ever heard the saying, there is someone for everyone? People usually say this after seeing the behavior of a person, and then they wonder how somebody can put up with them. Have you ever seen someone who stunning, and you wonder who they are married to?

One such person who comes to mind is Abigail. In 1 Samuel 25, we read about an encounter with a man named Nabal (literally means fool) and the scripture says,

"The man's name was Nabal, and his wife's
name was Abigail; she was a woman of good
understanding and beautiful. But the man was

rough and evil in his doings; he was a Calebite"
(1 Samuel 25:3, AMPC).

The story tells of the unfair treatment of the king's request and the king's swift reaction. In fact, King David is determined to wipe out all of the men in Abigail family.

"Now David had said, surely in vain have I protected all that this fellow has in the wilderness, so that nothing was missed of all that belonged to him; and he has repaid me evil for good. May God do so, and more also, to David if I leave of all who belong to him one male alive by morning" (1 Samuel 25:21-22, AMPC).

The wonderful thing about Abigail is that even though she lived under difficult conditions, it did not change her into a difficult person. The story goes on to say that she went before King David with great hospitality and saved her household. How many people would have taken the opportunity to let the King get rid of their problem? But this woman's husband, who did not earn or deserve her trust, was saved because of the integrity and honor of his wife. She also found great favor in the sight of the King because he said:

"Blessed be the Lord, the God of Israel, Who sent you this day to meet me. And blessed be your discretion and advice and blessed be you who have kept me today from blood guiltiness and from avenging myself with my own hand. For as the Lord, the God of Israel, lives, Who has prevented me from hurting you, if you had not hurried and come to meet me, surely by morning there would not have been left so much as one male to Nabal." (1 Samuel 25:32-34, AMPC).

So not only did Abigail action save her household, but she kept the King and his men from a grievous act. Has your action ever kept people from committing grievous act, or do you look on a situation and said, oh well? God expects us to be his representatives in the earth and, like Abigail, intercede on his behalf to right the wrongs that we can control.

Journal Page – Activity – Think of a time when you acted on behalf of someone who didn't deserve it. Then write how that action impacted your relationship with God.

_____

_____

_____

_____

_____

_____

_____

_____

_____

_____

_____

_____

_____

_____

_____

_____

_____

_____

She is Confident in Many Endeavors

"You must be the change you wish to see in the world."
– Mahatma Gandhi

We see this example in Mary, the mother of Jesus. As a young woman betrothed, we would say engaged but not yet married, Mary is the woman God chose to use as the mother of his son. According to scripture, the young and engaged Mary did not resist the instruction of the Angel but submitted her life to his instruction and the subsequent encounter with the Holy Ghost. Her response unlike her cousin-in-law and priest Zacharias was of faith and not of unbelief. She responded,

"I am the Lord's servant," Mary answered. "May your word to me be fulfilled." Then the angel left her." (Luke 1:38, NIV).

She was trained to trust God before she was married. You might say, sure, that was back then what about now? I don't have angels appearing to me. Oh, but you do. The scripture says,

"Do not forget to show hospitality to strangers, for by so doing some people have shown hospitality to angels without knowing it." (Hebrews 13:2, NIV).

The question will be if you received the message and then heard and adhered to what he spoke concerning the kingdom of God. If God challenged you with a life changing situation that put you in a position of embarrassment even though it would jeopardize your future, would you do as they did? They had to trust God and submit to His wisdom.

Journal Page – Activity – Define trust in your own words. Then answer the question, Do you Trust God?

_____

_____

_____

_____

_____

_____

_____

_____

_____

_____

_____

_____

_____

_____

_____

_____

_____

_____

_____

_____

_____

_____

_____

She Avoids Mistakes

"To avoid mistakes and regrets, always consult your wife before engaging in flirtation." – E.W. Howe

My parents named me Sandra which really means helper of Mankind. God knew even before I did that helping would be my natural and spiritual calling. Being a helper to your husband is not a box to be checked off on your task list. Helping extends from heart to heart. God made Eve as a companion to Adam. She was of mankind, and she was able to communicate, touch, comfort, and work alongside of him.

We have a great example of a united couple in the scripture in Aquila and Priscilla. They are such a good example of a married couple, that when we refer to those who minister with and to the Apostle Paul, we say their names together. In them, God shows how a woman can be equally used for the going forth of the gospel and continue to support and help her husband. I am sure that, in some of the difficult days of the early church, Priscilla had to assume duties that seemed like they belonged to her husband. In scripture, we learn that they made tents and that Paul joined in with them making them at night. Priscilla was no weakling. She was right in the fight, ministering the Gospel, working and taking care of home. The scripture even says that their home was a place for meetings. In this case, can you see how much Priscilla was trusted by her husband to have thing in order in the home, in spite of the fact that their business and ministry was there. She made decisions that kept her husband safe both in business and ministry. The perilous days of the early church was not a romantic story. In a labor of love, Priscilla had to truly understand her role along with Paul[18] and the early church, in preaching the same gospel that Jesus preached. Also bringing correction to those who had not understood the baptism of Jesus Christ.

The point of whether or not God uses women to correct, and lead is moot. The essence of the Bible shows that he always had and always will. Organized religion does not always adhere to God's leading. It can be full of man-made tradition, which hinders people from entering the Kingdom of God. Jesus said to the Pharisees' and religious leaders,

---

"But "Woe to you, teachers of the law and Pharisees, you hypocrites! You shut the door of the kingdom of heaven in people's faces. You yourselves do not enter, nor will you let those enter who are trying to" (Matthew 23:13 NIV).

So, this is not a license to stop going to church or worship services, for God is very serious about believers coming together[19]. I am saying that some of the standards did not come from or do not represent God's Kingdom.

---

[18] Acts 18:18 - 23
[19] Hebrews 10:25

Aquila was not the only woman in God's service as part of the servant leadership that is the church. Some married and some unmarried women have great responsibilities that God entrusts to them, since he has trained them to be jewels in his crown. According to scripture, many women followed Christ and had direct impact on his ministry.

> *"After this, Jesus traveled about from one town and village to another, proclaiming the good news of the kingdom of God. The Twelve were with him, and also some women who had been cured of evil spirits and diseases: Mary (called Magdalene) from whom seven demons had come out; Joanna the wife of Chuza, the manager of Herod's household; Susanna; and many others. These women were helping to support them out of their own means." (Luke 8:1-3 NIV).*

Just like then, God has equipped you to represent the Kingdom of Heaven, as you were predestined to do so.

> *"Even as [in His love] He chose us [actually picked us out for Himself as His own] in Christ*

before the foundation of the world, that we should be holy (consecrated and set apart for Him) and blameless in His sight, even above reproach, before Him in love. For He foreordained us (destined us, planned in love for us) to be adopted (revealed) as His own children through Jesus Christ, in accordance with the purpose of His will [because it pleased Him and was His kind intent]" (Ephesians 1: 4-5 AMPC).

Don't give any excuses that you are not the virtuous woman God called you to be. If your life has been full of attacks from the enemy like Mary Magdalene, then read the Bible, to see that you have power and authority that you have not discovered yet. God has a place for you to minister to the body of Christ as a servant leader, and he is making you into a vessel of honor.[20]

At the time of this writing, my husband and I have been married almost a half a century. Who would have thought it? I remember being in a lot of difficult situations, mostly during the first 15 years. One of those years, my husband worked for a plastic molding company. The work really did not suite him. For many reasons, he was inside when he really

---

[20] 2 Tim 2: 20-21

should be outside. The plastic mix made him sick, and he did not get along with certain personalities, especially his overbearing supervisors. His need and desire were warring against our need for the money he was making. It seemed like no other opportunities were available.

Going forward, I would listen to and observe my husband while we were on a trip. He was the type of person who took delight in driving from one state to another. Additionally, he always wants to be outside – fishing, hunting, and camping. To make a long story short, we eventually were presented with an opportunity to purchase a truck which we did from part of my invested money from work. That started MOF Express LLC, which is one of our current businesses and is over 20 plus years old. My ability to see his need to be in another career path and to encourage him in his natural ability allowed us to agree in more ways, which would not have been the case if he had stayed in a position where he was unhappy. It has affected our lives in a very positive way.

Journal Page – Activity – Look at your husband or a person who has great influence in your life and write a short job description of what you feel they would be best at. Discuss with them, in love, why you feel this way. Then come up with 3 action items that will help them to do something they will love to do and to avoid any bad action that they would encounter on a different track. This may not be an easy conversation to have!

_____

_____

_____

_____

_____

_____

_____

_____

_____

_____

_____

_____

_____

Changing Your Virtuality (Virtue Reality)

She Loves, Comfort and Encourages her Household

"Hardship often prepare ordinary people for an extraordinary destiny." – C.S. Lewis

One of my favorite singing groups of all time was the soulful and powerful team of Nick and Valarie Ashford. They were not only husband and wife but business partners, song writers and music producers. The most iconic song they wrote was, "Ain't No Mountain High Enough," originally performed by Tammy Terrell and Marvin Gaye. I once saw a documentary of them that quoted Valarie as saying that she came up with the song while they were driving through the city, and Nick said, "We call, 'Ain't No Mountain' the golden egg that landed us at Motown." Their public lives appeared to be solid, and like the virtuous woman, many people could see that Nick was blessed to have a wife who loved him out loud. It showed in their music and in the fidelity and length of their marriage. Upon Nick's death in 2011, people immediately ask Valerie how she was going to go on. Her response made out of love for him was "I had to let him go, he was tired." That part of love, the love of until death will we part that essence allows it to last past the temporary plane of this life, it will continue and be part of their interaction before God Our Father when all rewards are reconciled.[21]

---

[21] Matt 25:34

Changing Your Virtuality (Virtue Reality)

Not everyone has an idyllic marriage, friendship, or relationship. However, any man that can find a wife who understands him and endures with him through all the difficulties of this life, is blessed of God.

> *"He who finds a wife, finds what is good and receives favor from the Lord." (Proverbs 18:22 NIV)*

Some people might say that it is not necessary to be married to a person to have a good and lasting relationship. As I mentioned before, there are many stages that we as women encounter to become a pliable vessel of God. From being little girls, to teenagers, to young women, to mature women, to elders and senior counsels in our families and communities, we bear the responsibility of exhibiting the side of God that declares strength inside of beauty.

Therefore, every woman, whether she is Rehab the Harlot, Mary the mother of Jesus, Little Kim, Michelle Obama, Queen Mary I, or even Mother Teresa, has the unique ability of declaring the presence of God through feminine strength. Of course, not all women do this with dignity or morality, but that does not negate their God-given attributes.

There are many stories that I could cite to point out this particular attribute. I like to think that there are many women who make monumental differences in their husbands' lives. Not all such relationships are public or well known. I like to think of a few couples without the mention of names, like some pastors and their wives, even some Hollywood stars and their wives.

One of the most beautiful stories of a love match and subsequent love story was Ruth and Boaz. As we continue with Ruth as our example, I know many people have used this story to characterize Boaz as prince charming and Ruth as the loyal but desperate foreigner. But let's just open the side of the story that sometimes gets overlooked. Ruth – the widowed daughter-in-law of Naomi and close widowed cousin of Boaz – was not in any position of prominence. Once married, a Moabite, childless and forty years old. These attributes made her appear to be forsaken by God and less then valuable. In today's society, especially some of the more judgmental holy denominations, Ruth would have been gossiped about and judged, blamed, and stigmatized.

Mean girls would throw jabs at Ruth and say something like "you know, if Ruth had any sense, she should have gone back to her own home." and things like "what makes Ruth think she can come here and just throw herself at him" so on and so forth. Even in those days I'm sure that there were enough mean girls, socialites, neighbors, and relatives to give Ruth the feeling that somebody just didn't like her. In spite of the mean girl council Boaz tell Ruth *"...All the people of my town know that you are a woman of noble character"*.[22]

---

[22] Ruth 3:11 NIV

Boaz was a hard-working bachelor prince, and he may have been a widower and a father whose children were all deceased.[23] He worked and patrolled his thrashing floor like a regular laborer. The pair got together after some bargaining and negotiating with people who had an interest in Naomi's land and future. However, the story goes on to show only a sketching of the relationship that would eventually be included in the linage of King David and, ultimately, the Messiah Jesus. All the rules and cultural stigmas that surround this story are softened by the incredible circumstances in which God orchestrates this relationship. The trusting part of their relationship did not only come from their interaction, but also from what Boaz had heard from the overseer of his harvest and the people of the town, that Ruth was a virtuous woman. Eventually, Boaz realized that Ruth has shown him great favor and kindness to marry him and not a younger man.

Boaz also saw the virtuous nature of Ruth and her honorable behavior, which helped him to fall in line with God's plan, and he accepted Ruth's counsel that she should be his wife.[24] At the end of the book, the praise for Naomi is a song at the birth of Ruth's son Obed, and the song depicts the monumental significance of Boaz wisdom. So many look on and saw the great benefit he gained by making Ruth his wife. With all her heart and strength, she submitted to the law, the wisdom of her mother-in-law, and culture of the land, eventually supporting her

---

[23] See https://torah.org/learning/ruth-class41/#
[24] Ruth 3:9,12-13 NIV

commitment to Naomi and allowing Boaz regard for her to fulfill God's promise

Journal Page – Activity – Write down one of your most difficult challenges that you had while believing God for one of your deepest desires. Then comment on how God used this to make you the person you are.

_____

_____

_____

_____

_____

_____

_____

_____

_____

_____

_____

_____

_____

_____

_____

_____

_____

_____

Conclusion

In Conclusion, **<u>Change</u>** can be as simple as looking at things from God's perspective and allowing your will to align with His will for your life. Then as you live according to his word, you can experience the manifestation of the scripture below,

"Therefore, I tell you, whatever you ask for in prayer, believe that you have received it, and it will be yours." (Mark 11:24 NIV)

Journal Page – Activity: Review all your comments notated in this journal. Then write a personal prayer.

_____

_____

_____

_____

_____

_____

_____

_____

_____

_____

_____

_____

_____

_____

I am excited to inform you that this publication is the first of a 5-book series regarding the revelation of the Proverbs 31 woman and your identification with her. As you read, ponder, and identify with her, I believe your miracle of healing, illumination and revelation will become abundantly clear. I trust that the abilities, which you have been blessed with, will become the evidence of God's presence in your life and affirmation to even clearer instructions regarding your future endeavors.

Peace

Sandra Patrick

Books in this Series: Changing your Virtuality (Virtue Reality)

Book 1. Authentication

Book 2. Transformation

Book 3. Dedication

Book 4. Application

Book 5. Production/Jubilation

Appendix: 20 Characteristics

Comprehensive Overview of the Proverbs 31 woman

"You compensate every man according to his works." (Psalm 62:12)

The following outline list the characteristics of the woman described in Proverbs 31:10-31. This is the interpretation God has revealed to me so we can understand in today's language the action and accomplishments of this woman.

1. She is intelligent, capable, virtuous, spiritually discerning, able to choose the good portion, resourceful and industrious. Her presence is uniquely desirable, and her worth is not measured by the current market rate of precious stones, for she has proven to be much more valuable.

2. Her relationship with her husband or with God, if she is single has been developed such that he totally trusts her decisions to bring honor to him and their household. His confidence in her has been solidified through her ability to love, guide, and support his decisions in many endeavors. She helps him to choose honest and excellent ways to avoid mistakes. Her ability to love, comfort and encourage him is done with all her strength and causes him to be the envy of many, as they see that she is very good to him.

3. Though she has many skills, she chooses the projects that she can start herself and works them until they can be delegated to her helpers (children, servants, employees, and contractors).

4. She is skilled in using many avenues and mediums of exchange and finds the right market to fill her household with the necessary and desired goods.

5. She prays without ceasing, seeking God for wisdom on how to operate her household as well as her many enterprises.

6. She is wise in making commitments because she considers her current duties. Being faithful regarding them, she seeks wisdom from God on how to add to her already fruitful and prosperous enterprises. Her new endeavors prove her efficiency and shows off her time management skills.

7. Her strength does not detract from her feminine beauty because it is the evidence of her diligence to adhere to the presence of God in her earthly temple by keeping her mind, body and soul as trained as any earthly military personnel.

8. Her business acumen, both spiritually and naturally, far supersedes others, and she guarantees that all her services will be performed in an excellent manner. She is more diligent than any CEO, overseer, or watchman. She is vigilant all

through the night to detect, expose, pray and plan for any difficulties. She endures hardship like a good soldier.

9. She embraces technology, which allows her to be productive and practical, resulting in supernatural results during the day.

10. Her superabundance allows many needs to be met to those who lack resources, whether spiritually or naturally. The members of her household own well-made clothes and are prepared for any season. She gives generously to the poor, which results in perpetual blessings for her household.

11. She chooses the best durable, practical, and beautiful materials for all of her household furnishings.

12. Her presence always reflects her status and the way she wears her dresses as a representative of her household and the Kingdom of God.

13. When she sells her products or services, it always enhances the life of her customers, and they are delighted with the results.

14. Her integrity has been tested and proven. She and her family live in a constant state of celebration because they are spiritually, financially, socially, mentally, and physically

poised to face the challenges of today and for the days to come.

15. Her native tongue is that of the Kingdom of God. She speaks in love and generosity, laced strategically with the words of her heavenly Father.

16. She supervises her own household and fills it with positive energy, godly worship and validating praise. She does not allow unfruitful relationships to monopolize her day.

17. Her children obey and honor her cheerfully following instruction with the understanding that they are blessed. Her children tell all their friends that they have the best mother in the world. Her husband is a constant encouragement to her, telling everyone that she is one in a million.

18. There is no question that she is a rare person with impeccable manners and of excellent character. Everyone who sees her is impressed by her presence and knows that she is an ambassador of peace and love.

19. She is not defined by her outward beauty, excellent speech, and diplomacy since those things can be tarnished with time. She is praised for her consistent truthfulness, sincere,

uncompromising worship, and her dedication to God's people.

20. The results of her efforts are spoken of throughout the region, and her profits are poured back into her own hands.

Changing Your Virtuality (Virtue Reality)

Made in the USA
Middletown, DE
26 May 2022